I0459721

HELP!
Easter Bunny is in Trouble

By Effin Older

Bunny Farm Press
Chickamauga, GA USA

HELP! EASTER BUNNY IS IN TROUBLE By Effin Older
Published by Bunny Farm Press, an imprint of Three Ravens
Publishing
threeravenspublishing@gmail.com
P O Box 851, Chickamauga, Ga 30707
https://www.threeravenspublishing.com
Copyright © 2025 by Effin Older

Publishers Note: This is a work of fiction. Names, characters, places,
and incidents are a product of the author's imagination. Locales and
public names are sometimes used for atmospheric purposes. Any
resemblance to actual people, living or dead, or to businesses,
companies, events, institutions, or locales is completely coincidental.

Credits:
HELP! EASTER BUNNY IS IN TROUBLE was written by Effin
Older

HELP! EASTER BUNNY IS IN TROUBLE by: Effin Older
/Bunny Farm Press-Three Ravens Publishing – 1st edition, 2025

Ebook ISBN: 978-1-966507-09-3
Trade Paperback ISBN: 978-1-966507-10-9
Hardback ISBN: 978-1-966507-11-6

Dedication

This is dedicated to

Jules

and

Willow and Amber

Best. Editors. Ever!

Table of Contents

CHAPTER 1

In a little cottage in Lilac Village, the Twinkles were painting Easter eggs.

Mr. Twinkle painted two bright blue stars on his egg.

Mrs. Twinkle painted a bee buzzing a sunflower on her egg.

Four-year-old Washington Twinkle painted something on his egg, but only he could tell what it was. Then he sat back in his chair with his thumb in his mouth and his finger in his nose. He studied the egg and grinned. "Me yike."

"Say *I like*, Washington, *I like*," said his big sister, Tulip, as she put the finishing touches on her egg. She painted the sun shining on a patch of red and yellow flowers. A little, pink-nosed bunny peeked out from under one of the flowers.

Mr. Twinkle looked over at Tulip's egg. "That's a fancy painting for a seven-year-old."

Tulip rolled her eyes and clucked her tongue. "Excuse me, Dad, I'm seven-going-on-eight, remember?"

Mr. Twinkle chuckled. "A thousand pardons."

"Excuse *me*, you two," Mrs. Twinkle said, putting down her paintbrush. "Tomorrow's the big Easter egg hunt. The Easter Bunny must be crazy-busy right now getting ready to hide eggs all around the village and across the meadow."

Tulip clapped her hands. "Oooh, I can't wait! Last year, I found not one, not two, but *three* eggs. And one had chocolate buttons inside!" She licked her lips. "Yum. Extra chocolate for me!"

At the sound of the word *chocolate*, Truffle, the Twinkles' floppy-eared basset hound, woofed.

Tulip wagged her finger at Truffle. "Not for you," she warned. "Chocolate's *bad* for dogs."

"*Good* fo' me," said Washington, pulling his wet thumb out of his mouth and his finger out of his nose. He patted himself on the stomach. "Yum, yum, yummy in tum, tum, tummy."

"I'm sure the Easter Bunny will leave something delicious for both of you," said Mrs. Twinkle. She patted Truffle on the head. "And don't worry, we won't forget you. We'll be sure you get something doggy-licious, too."

She turned to Tulip and Washington. "Now, quickly, you two finish your eggs and off to bed. You want to be bright-eyed and bushy-tailed for the hunt tomorrow morning."

Washington stood up and checked between his legs. His bottom lip began to quiver. "Me no bushy tail," he whimpered.

Tulip let out a big sigh. "Oh, Washington, Mom doesn't mean you need a *real* bushy tail. She just means you need to go to bed early so you'll have lots of energy to look for Easter eggs. Right, Mom?"

"Mrs. Twinkle nodded. "Exactly."

Washington painted two more squiggly lines on his egg. Then he sat back in his chair, stuck his thumb in his mouth and his finger in his nose. He smiled at his egg and nodded. "Me yike," he said again.

"I think they're *all* beautiful," said Mrs. Twinkle. "Let's leave them here on the table for the paint to dry."

"Me dry in box," Washington mumbled. He scurried off to his bedroom and returned a minute later holding a little wooden box with a gold lock. He took off a chain he wore around his neck. Five little keys dangled from the chain. Each key fit a box where he kept his special things—shiny sea shells, miniature race cars, animal-shaped erasers, and old rusty keys. Washington picked the smallest key, which was no bigger than a bumble bee, and unlocked the wooden box. He opened the lid and carefully placed the egg inside.

"Better leave the lid open," Mr. Twinkle advised. "Otherwise, it might not dry."

Washington nodded and hitched the chain of keys back around his neck.

While Mr. and Mrs. Twinkle put the finishing touches on their eggs, and while Tulip and Washington slipped into their PJs, and while Truffle turned four circles before settling down in his comfy donut-shaped bed, little did they know that …

HELP! Easter Bunny is in Trouble

CHAPTER 2

Little did they know that, in the green meadow surrounding Lilac Village, another family was also preparing for Easter. It was the family of Bentley and Bella Biscotti. *Sir* Bentley Biscotti. He became *Sir* Bentley when the Queen of the Fairies knighted him for all his good works. She'd hung a shiny gold medal shaped like a rabbit's paw around his neck. He never took it off. From that day on, Sir Bentley became Sir Bentley **OEB**—the **O**fficial **E**aster **B**unny. He was the one and only bunny *officially* in charge of delivering Easter eggs to children around the world. It was a great honor.

Sir Bentley and his beautiful wife, Bella, lived in B&B Warren—B for Bentley and B for Bella. Other bunny families lived in the warren, too. (A warren is an underground home with lots and lots of rabbit-size rooms and rabbit-size tunnels.)

Every year, under Sir Bentley's watchful eye, the rabbits who lived in B&B Warren made loads of chocolate Easter eggs. Each egg was tightly wrapped in thick, sparkly paper to make it easy for children to spot and, more importantly, impossible for dogs to eat. (Chocolate is bad for dogs. It's also bad for cats and monkeys and foxes. Even bunnies shouldn't eat chocolate, but they're *great* at making it, and they *love* giving it away.)

Right now, Sir Bentley was in trouble. As he was zipping around the warren on his electric scooter, suddenly and without warning, the front wheel popped right off! Sir Bentley went flying, head over ears over cotton tail, and landed in a heap on the dirt floor of the warren. He quickly realized he'd injured not one, not two, not three, but all four of his paws!

Luckily, Bella saw Sir Bentley's crash and hurried to his side. She helped him into a comfortable chair and offered him a cup of chamomile tea. Once Sir Bentley was feeling better, he looked more closely at his scooter. "Hmmm, that's curious," he muttered.

"What's curious?" Bella asked her husband.

"Hmmm. Looks like there's a screw missing from the front wheel."

"How do you think that happened, Benny?"

Sir Bentley shook his long, straight-up bunny ears. "Beats me, Bella. Maybe I didn't—"

"The missing screw!" Bella interrupted. "That's why you took such a tumble. Dear me, dear me." She sighed. "The timing couldn't be worse! We have the Easter egg hunt tomorrow and dozens of chocolate eggs still to make." She sighed again. "I could sit right down and cry."

"Now, now, my dear, there's no need for tears especially if ... " Benny paused, "if I can put *you* in charge this year."

"What? Me!" exclaimed Bella. "*You're* the Easter Bunny, not me."

"But you've always been right by my side. You know exactly how everything works." Sir Bentley patted his wife's soft furry shoulder. "This year, I'll be right by *your* side."

Bella thought for a minute then, suddenly, she sat up straight on her hind legs. Her black nose twitched. "I've just had a thought. A terrible, terrible thought. Do you think someone might have fiddled with the screw when you left your scooter outside at the charging station?"

"Of course not! Who on Earth would want to hurt *me*, the **OEB**? I'm sure it was just a silly accident. Could have happened to anyone." Sir Bentley hugged his wife. "So, this year it's up to you, my dear. What do you say?"

Bella took a deep breath and let it out slowly. "I'll do my best. We can't disappoint the children. The Easter egg hunt must go on." She smiled at her husband. "Luckily, we have our children to help."

There were 11 Biscotti children. There was Blueberry and Blackberry (the first set of twins), Bacon, Burger, and Burrito (the first set of triplets), Broccoli and Beet (the second set of twins), Banana, Brownie, and Biscuit (also triplets), and the youngest of all, Baby Baklava. Unlike her brothers and sisters who were white with blue eyes, Baby Baklava was brown with brown eyes. She was the youngest and smallest bunny in the warren. She was also the most curious.

All 11 bunnies had been quietly listening to their parents. "We'll help! We'll help!" they shouted, "and we'll get all our friends in the warren to help, too."

"Great idea," agreed Sir Bentley. "Off you go."

So, while Sir Bentley sat down to rest his aching paws, and while Bella slipped on her special Easter apron decorated with brightly painted eggs, and while the 11 Biscotti bunnies rounded up their buddies to help, little did they all know that …

HELP! Easter Bunny is in Trouble

CHAPTER 3

Little did they all know that, deep in the dark, shadowy, pine forest that surrounded the green meadow and Lilac Village, another kind of family was also preparing for the Easter egg hunt.

Inside a large dome, a short, chubby troll stared at himself in a cracked, door-size mirror. The troll wore a red cowboy hat. His red jacket and pants matched his cowboy hat. A belt with a big brass buckle held up his baggy pants. His long white beard and curly white hair were made of pillow stuffing.

The troll studying himself in the mirror was none other than Mugsy Maldoom. He had recently moved from the North Pole to the dark pine forest. He'd arrived just *before* Easter, just *before* the big Easter egg hunt, and just *before* Sir Bentley Biscotti's terrible scooter tumble.

Crowded around the troll were dozens of pint-size trolls who looked just like him.

They were Mugsy's mogsters. Like Mugsy, they all wore red cowboy hats, red jackets and pants, and white pillow-stuffing beards. All except one. *That* pint-size troll had a brown nose, a brown cowboy hat, and a brown pillow-stuffing beard. His name was Ralph. He was the youngest and smallest mogster. He was also the most friendly, the most helpful, and the most adventurous of all the mogsters.

You might remember that, last Christmas, Mugsy had not been one bit friendly to Tulip, Washington, and Truffle. He'd trapped them in a net, like flies in a spider's web. He'd been even less friendly to Santa. The troll had tried to stop Santa from delivering his presents on Christmas Eve. Mugsy's plan was to ruin Santa's job, once and for all, by making *fake* toys for Christmas. *Children will love me and* my *toys more than Santa and* his *toys*, he'd said to himself. *It'll be "Good-bye, Santa!"*

But his plan didn't work. And, now, trouble-making Mugsy Maldoom was up to no-good again. He blew a kiss to the troll in the mirror. *I'll be the best, most-loved Easter Bunny ever!*

When Mugsy left the North Pole, he'd brought his mogsters, and he'd also brought Mugsy Maldoom's Marvelous Mogadome. The Mogadome was a shimmering, star-studded dome. It had four giant M's along the top. The M's stood for Mugsy Maldoom's Marvelous Mogadome. So, now, here he was, getting ready to carry out his secret scheme—his scheme to spoil Sir Bentley's eggs and become the official, most-loved Easter Bunny ever.

His eggs would *look* like Sir Bentley's eggs.

His eggs would *feel* like Sir Bentley's eggs.

But, would his eggs *taste* like Sir Bentley's eggs?

NO, THEY WOULDN'T!

That was his big secret plan.

"Once the children taste *my* eggs with *my* secret ingredients, they'll never want another one of Bentley's again." He sniggered. "That will make *me*, Mugsy Maldoom, more loved than *Sir* Bentley. Every Easter, children will beg for *my* scrumptious, special-ingredient eggs. I'll be famous! More famous than Santa! More famous than Mickey Mouse! Even more famous than the Tooth Fairy!

When he first arrived in the dark pine forest, Mugsy spotted Sir Bentley's electric scooter. It sat outside the warren, being charged. "Ah ha!" Mugsy chuckled, rubbing his hands together. The scooter gave him a great idea.

Meanwhile …

CHAPTER 4

Meanwhile, stacks and stacks of sparkly-wrapped Easter eggs (some with chocolate buttons inside) now filled all the rooms and all the tunnels in the B&B Warren. Every egg had an **OEB** sticker on it to prove it came from the **O**fficial **E**aster **B**unny. There were so many eggs, some were even spilling out of the entrance to the warren.

Bella Biscotti wiped her sweaty forehead with her paw. "I think the job is finally done," she said. "There are plenty of eggs for every child to find at least one or ... if they're lucky, maybe two or even three."

"You've saved the day, my dear," said Sir Bentley. "Thank goodness the Easter egg hunt will go on as usual."

After hours and hours of work, Bella was almost too weary to smile at her husband, but she managed a little nod. "The sun will soon come up, Benny. It's time for you to organize our children and their friends to get busy hiding eggs."

"No problemo," said Sir Bentley. "Just because I can't ride my scooter doesn't mean I can't supervise." He called to his 11 children and their friends. "Fill up your wagons and your wheelbarrows and your backpacks. You have to work fast before daybreak. We don't want anyone to catch you hiding eggs."

After a mad scramble in the warren with bunnies running to and fro' and fro' and to, they were ready to go. Out of the warren streamed bunnies by the dozen. Each one carried eggs by the dozen.

Although there was almost no light to guide them, soon the bunnies had hidden every last egg in Lilac Village and the green meadow. For good measure, they even hid a few in the dark, shadowy pine forest. The bunnies were so busy scurrying here and there that no one noticed something strange. Something strange in the pine forest.

Almost no one noticed.

Baby Baklava noticed.

She noticed a large dome hidden among the trees. *I've never seen that before,* she thought. *I wonder what it is.* Being a very, very curious bunny, she wanted to investigate but, then, she remembered her mother's words: "You're the baby of the family. Promise to stay close to your older brothers and sisters. You don't want to get into any trouble."

Baby Baklava had promised, and she meant to keep her promise, but … but her curiosity was growing by the second, and her paws were steering her straight for the mysterious dome.

Maybe just a little peek was Baby Baklava's first thought.

She took one hop. She stopped and looked around. The other bunnies were so busy hiding eggs, they weren't paying attention to her.

I'll be quick like a bunny was her second thought.

She was about to hop another hop when she had her third thought. *But ... but I promised Mama I'd stay close to—"*

Baby Baklava didn't get to finish her third thought because, at that moment, she heard her Biscotti brothers and sisters shout, "Done! Everybody back to the warren, ASAP!"

With empty wheelbarrows, empty wagons, and empty backpacks, the bunnies scampered home. Not one egg was left to be hidden.

Baby Baklava had no choice. She had to follow her brothers and sisters. Now, she would never know where the mysterious dome had come from and why it was in the dark pine forest.

"Well done," said Sir Bentley who was waiting at the entrance of B&B Warren. "*Very* well done. I'm proud of you all."

Bella stepped out from behind her husband. "And as a special Easter thank-you, I've prepared your very favorite food … plus an Easter treat."

"What is it?" the bunnies shouted. "Tell us! Tell us!"

"Come see for yourself." Bella motioned for the bunnies to follow her deep into the warren. "Now close your eyes. No peeking. That goes for you, too, Baby B." Baby Baklava was so curious she covered one eye and only half-covered the other. Among the rest of the bunnies, not a peek could be seen, and not a peep could be heard. "Now, open!"

Piled in front of the bunnies was the biggest, greenest, sweetest-smelling stack of hay they'd ever seen. And on the very top, sticking out like birthday candles on a cake, was the special Easter treat—broccoli! Bunches and bunches of the freshest, tenderest, most succulent broccoli in the whole world!

"Dig in," said Sir Bentley. "You've earned it. Your hard work is done until next Easter."

As much as she loved sweet, green hay and tender, succulent broccoli, Baby Baklava didn't dig in. She had something else on her mind. Something she was very curious about. Something that troubled her.

She looked around. Sir Bentley and Bella had disappeared into their bedroom to take a nap. The other bunnies were so busy chomping on their tasty treats that no one noticed when the brown bunny tiptoed back down one of the many tunnels in B&B Warren and out to the front entrance. She had not forgotten what she'd seen in the dark pine forest. And her curiosity had grown bigger and bigger. As Baby B sat in the entrance to the warren, four questions spun round and round in her head:

Why was there a dome hidden among the trees?

Where did it come from?

Did anyone live there?

Were they friendly?

And there was one last question Baby B asked herself. It was the most important question of all: What about her promise to her mother?

There was no doubt about it. Baby Baklava was facing a tough decision: Should she keep her promise and risk bursting with curiosity, or should she break it and solve the mystery?

Meanwhile …

HELP! Easter Bunny is in Trouble

CHAPTER 5

Meanwhile, as the very hungry Biscotti bunnies and their friends were munching on their sweet, sweet treats, Mugsy and his gang of mogsters were racing against time. And time was quickly running out. Soon, the sun would start slowly peeking above the horizon, and the day would break. Mugsy needed the dark of night to carry out his devious Easter deed.

Since arriving in the dark pine forest, Mugsy had been very busy. Here's what he did:

Job 1

He changed from looking like Santa (sort of) to looking like Sir Bentley (sort of). He now had tall, white, straight-up bunny ears poking through his red cowboy hat. Instead of a red jacket and pants, his suit was made of white, stick-on cotton balls with one big cotton ball tail. A wide belt around his extremely tubby tummy held up his pants.

Instead of a red cherry nose, he had a black olive nose. He still wore shiny, black, Santa boots.

Mugsy also changed all his mogster trolls to look just like him, right down to their white cotton ball tails and shiny black boots...

All the mogsters except for one. *This* pint-size troll had brown, straight-up ears, a brown nose, and a brown bunny suit made of brown stick-on cotton balls. He had one big, brown, cotton ball tail. It was Ralph, the smallest, youngest, and most adventurous mogster.

Job 2

Mugsy snuck over to B&B Warren and stole the screw on the front wheel of Sir Bentley's electric scooter. "Take that!" he sneered. "Hoppy riding! Hee hee hee."

Job 3

Inside the Mogadome, Mugsy turned on his marvelous egg-making machines. Each one was as big as a refrigerator and shaped like an egg. The machines had doors with reach-through bars and were covered in gems—sparkling rubies, glimmering emeralds, shimmering diamonds, and shiny gold. *No one but me will ever guess they're* **fake** *gems*, Mugsy snickered.

Mugsy and his mogsters made loads and loads of sparkly-wrapped eggs. On the outside, the eggs looked like Sir Bentley's eggs. But on the inside? Not so much.

Job 4

Under the cover of darkness, before the sun peeked over the horizon, dozens of mogsters crept out of the Mogadome. Each one carried a basket filled with Mugsy's special-formula Easter eggs. Mugsy ordered his mogsters to pick up every last one of Sir Bentley's eggs and put one of *his* in its place. He chuckled a wicked chuckle. "We'll see which eggs the children love—Smarty-Pants Bentley Biscotti's or Marvellous Mugsy Maldoom's."

The mogsters did exactly as they were told. Soon, their baskets were filled to the brims with the eggs Bella Biscotti had so lovingly made. Then, Mugsy rounded up his mogsters and headed back to the Mogadome. "Quick! Dump Sir Bentley's eggs into my storage bins, lock the doors, and bring me the keys. We don't want to leave one single clue for those pesky Biscotti bunnies … or anyone else who might come sneaking around."

The mogsters dumped Sir Bentley's eggs into the bins, locked the doors, and gave the keys to Mugsy. He patted one of the bins. "The eggs will be 100% safe in you. Mwahhahaha."

Little did Mugsy know that not *all* the mogsters dumped *all* their eggs or gave *all* their keys to Mugsy. One mogster tucked one egg, just one, under his red cowboy hat. It smelled so deliciously chocolatey that Ralph couldn't resist. *Nobody will miss one little egg*, he said to himself. *I'll eat it when no one's looking.*

But that's not all Ralph tucked under his red cowboy hat. *Mugsy won't miss one little key,* he added under his breath ... *in case I get hungry for another chocolate egg.*

Job 5

Mugsy slipped off his shiny black boots, sat down on a rickety old rocking chair and put up his feet on a pile of grungy pillows. Then, he knighted himself. How? By hanging a smelly old sock around his neck.

He patted himself on the back. "I declare *me* the **O**fficial **E**aster **B**unny. *Me, Sir* Mugsy Maldoom. Wait until all those bratty kids get a taste of my deeeee-licious, secret-formula eggs. They'll never go back to plain, boring ol' chocolate again."

Then he and his exhausted mogsters fell into a deep, snorefully sleep. Little did Mugsy know that ...

HELP! Easter Bunny is in Trouble

CHAPTER 6

Little did Mugsy know that one mogster couldn't sleep. This mogster tried everything. He tossed and turned, and he turned and tossed. He drank a glass of warm spinach juice, he counted raccoons, he sang the alphabet song six times, he drank another glass of warm spinach juice, and he counted more raccoons.

Poor Ralph.

Like all the other mogsters, he had helped make Mugsy's special-formula Easter eggs.

Like all the other mogsters, he had helped with the big swap-a-roo of Sir Bentley's eggs for Mugsy's special-formula eggs.

Unlike all the other mogsters, Ralph was wide awake.

Why was Ralph wide awake?

Because he had a secret.

Ralph worried that, if his secret was found out, it would mean trouble. *Big* trouble.

Quietly, he slipped out of bed, past Mugsy and the other snoring mogsters. Once outside, he climbed up onto the roof of the Mogadome. Even though it was still quite dark, he thought he spotted something. Something zig-zagging here and there in the meadow.

Was he seeing things?

He rubbed his eyes. Was he dreaming?

He looked again. The thing had four short legs, two long floppy ears, and a wagging tail. It had its nose to the ground and went sniff-sniff, woof-woof.

I'd better keep an eye on this, he said to himself. *It could mean trouble.* Ralph settled down on his cotton-ball tail … to watch and to wait.

Meanwhile …

CHAPTER 7

Meanwhile, in Lilac Village, a nose twitched. It twitched again. It was a nose in the Twinkle household. It was the nose belonging to the occupant of the comfy, donut-shaped bed. It was Truffle. Truffle's nose was twitching.

Like all dogs, Truffle could smell about 40 times better than people. He could even smell smells that were far away, not right under his nose. What's more, like all dogs, Truffle was especially curious about *new* smells. New smells were exciting. They were exciting enough to wake the basset hound from a deep sleep and start his nose a-twitching.

And that's just what was happening now.

After three more twitches, Truffle scrambled out of his bed, squeezed through his dog door, and trotted into Lilac Village. As he trotted, his nose skimmed the ground. He dashed here and there, there and here. Sniff-sniff. Sniff-sniff. The smell was different from anything he'd ever smelled before and, because it was different, he wanted to find it. He *had* to find it.

Truffle sniffed all around the Village, all around the meadow, and even a few steps into the dark pine forest. He followed the smell. It was coming from sparkly wrapped, egg-shaped things hidden in tall grasses, behind trees, under benches, and in flower beds. As Truffle sniffed, three questions puzzled his doggy brain:

One: Am I smelling something good to eat, like a burger?

Two: Or something good to chase, like a ball?

Three: Or something good to chew, like a bone?

There was only one way to find out. Truffle opened his mouth wide and bit into one of the sparkly wrapped things. But he didn't chew.

He didn't swallow.

He spat out that nasty thing.

He rubbed his nose with his paw.

He shook his head from side to side.

He made sneezy noises.

Then, suddenly, as if he'd been stung on the tip of his nose by a bumble bee, he sprang backwards. He didn't know what he had tasted, but his doggy brain told him three things:

One: No, it wasn't something good to eat.

Two: No, it wasn't something good to chase.

Three: No, it wasn't something good to chew.

As fast as his short, basset-hound legs could run—which isn't all that fast—he left the icky thing on the ground and headed straight for home. He was nearly there when he spotted a hole in the ground. It was half-hidden behind a clump of bushes.

Truffle was as curious about holes as he was about new smells. He stopped and poked his nose into the hole. He sniffed. He woofed. He dug around the hole. He sniffed and poked and dug and woofed again.

Little did Truffle know that his nose was poking into the entrance of the B&B Warren. Little did he also know that, just moments before, Baby Baklava had been watching him! As Truffle got closer to where she was sitting, Baby B had scampered back into the safety of the warren. She shook in terror as she watched Truffle's nose poke, poke, poke into the entrance.

After a few more pokes, several more digs, and a lot of sniffs, Truffle, fed up with trying to squeeze his chunky body into the hole, removed his nose and made his way home. All this time, he had no idea he'd been spotted. He had no idea that a very, very curious bunny named Baby Baklava and an equally curious mogster named Ralph, had been watching his every move in the meadow.

Meanwhile …

HELP! Easter Bunny is in Trouble

CHAPTER 8

Meanwhile, now that the poking nose had disappeared, Baby Baklava hopped cautiously back to the entrance of B&B Warren. Behind her, she could hear the other bunnies chattering about the yummy green hay and the delicious broccoli. She was a little sorry she wasn't enjoying the special treats herself, but she had something more exciting on her mind.

It was big.

It was round.

It was mysterious.

Baby Baklava loved a mystery. The dome hidden in the dark pine forest was a big, round mystery. As she sat there, looking across the meadow, she started to get bunny bumps. She always got bunny bumps when she was unsure about what to do. She was unsure *now*. Should she go back into the warren and enjoy yummy broccoli, or should she try to solve the mystery of the dome? To help her decide, Baby B asked herself the same questions she'd asked herself when she first spotted the dome:

Why was it there?

Where did it come from?

Did anyone live there?

Were they friendly?

Most important of all, should she break her promise to her mother about not wandering off by herself?

It was this last question that brought on Baby Baklava's bunny bumps. Why? Because she was about to do just that— break her promise.

With her heart pounding, Baby B looked right, then left, then straight ahead. There was just enough light in the sky to see across the meadow and into the pine forest. If she stood on her tippy toes, she could just make out the top of the mysterious dome. *If I hop really fast, I can check out the dome and race back before it gets light. If the dome isn't friendly, I'll warn everyone. Then, they'll see what a brave little bunny I am, and they won't get mad at me for breaking my promise.*

Baby Baklava took a deep breath and hopped her first hop.

Meanwhile …

HELP! Easter Bunny is in Trouble

CHAPTER 9

Meanwhile, inside the little cottage in Lilac Village, Mr. and Mrs. Twinkle, Tulip Twinkle, and Washington Twinkle were still snuggled in their beds, dreaming about Easter bunnies and Easter eggs. No one heard the flip, flap, flip of Truffle's dog door as he squeezed back through it and padded into Tulip's bedroom. After three failed leaps, he finally made it the fourth time onto her bed. In another leap, he was eyeballing her nose.

He yipped.

Tulip didn't wake up.

He yipped again.

She still didn't wake up.

He licked her nose.

That did it! Tulip's eyes popped wide open. "What're you doing, Truffle? You scared me!" She sat up, rubbed her eyes, and looked around. "It's not time to get up; go back to bed."

Truffle didn't move. He yipped and licked her nose again. This time, Tulip jerked back. "Eewww! Your breath stinks!" She scrunched up her nose and wiped her face on her pajama sleeve. "Where have you been? What have you been eating? Eewww!"

Truffle jumped off the bed and scampered to the door. He twirled around. He sat down. He stared at Tulip. He twirled around again. Yip, yip, yip.

"Okay, I get it," Tulip muttered. She knew exactly what Truffle was doing—yipping, twirling around, sitting down, yipping, twirling around, sitting down always meant one thing—*follow me, Tulip, follow me.*

"Stop yipping, Truffle," she whispered, sliding off the bed. "You'll wake up Washington."

Too late.

Washington sat up in his bed. "Easter Bunny come?" he asked. "Me take a yook."

"It's too early, Washington. Go back to sleep," Tulip said softly. "Truffle's trying to tell me something. I'll be right back."

"Twuffle tell me, too," Washington said, tossing off the blanket.

Tulip sighed. "Oh, alright, but be quiet. We don't want to wake up Mom and Dad."

Truffle turned in circles as he waited for Tulip and Washington to follow him out of the bedroom. Then he led them down the hall and up to the front door. "Wait a minute, Truffle," Tulip whispered. "We need our jackets."

The basset hound sat impatiently by his dog door, watching Tulip and her brother slip their jackets over their PJs. Tulip tied a red-plaid scarf around Truffle's neck.

"Ready," Tulip said.

"Not weddy." Washington grabbed his Easter egg from the box on the kitchen table and stuffed it into his pocket. He grinned. "All dwy. Me yike. weddy, Tooyip."

Tulip patted Truffle's head. "Lead the way, Truffle."

Truffle didn't need to be told twice. Before Tulip had a chance to open the door, the floppy-eared hound disappeared through his dog door. Tulip and Washington followed through the people door.

"What is it, Truffle? Why are you getting me up so early?"

Truffle dashed ahead, turned around to make sure Tulip was following, then dashed ahead again. As Tulip watched, Truffle sniffed.

He sniffed behind trees.

He sniffed under benches

He sniffed in flower beds.

He sat down in a flower bed. He waited for Tulip and Washington to catch up.

"What are you smelling, Truffle?"

With his paw, Truffle rolled out a sparkly-wrapped egg. He rolled it next to Tulip's foot. Then, with his eyes fixed on Tulip, he sat down.

Before she could pick up the egg next to her foot, Washington grabbed it. "Yook! Easter egg!" He held it close to his face. He turned it round and round. He started to unwrap it when, suddenly, he dropped it to the ground. "Yucky! Icky yucky egg!"

"What?" Tulip cried. "What are you talking about? Easter eggs aren't yucky."

Tears rolled down Washington's chubby cheeks. "Stinky egg. Me no yike!"

Tulip picked up the egg her little brother had dropped.

It *looked* like a beautiful Easter egg.

It *felt* like a beautiful Easter egg.

It *smelled* like a … "Ewww! It *is* stinky! Just like your breath, Truffle!"

While Tulip was smelling the egg, Truffle rolled several more to her. She picked up each one, sniffed, and dropped them like hot potatoes. "Oh, no! They're all horrible!" She rubbed Truffle's head. "You *were* trying to tell me something. Now I get it." She held back tears. "It's almost time for the Easter egg hunt, and there's something really wrong with the eggs!"

Meanwhile …

CHAPTER 10

Meanwhile, in another part of the meadow, Baby Baklava had made up her mind. She took another hop. *I have to find out if the dome is friendly. If it isn't, I'll warn everyone.* Even though she was the youngest Biscotti Bunny, this was her chance to show she was the bravest.

Baby B continued hopping through the tall grass. She stopped for a moment to rest and look around. She was about to start off again when she noticed something in the distance … something that looked familiar.

It was a dog. The same dog that had tried to squeeze into the warren. And this time it wasn't alone. It was with two people.

Suddenly, Baby Baklava didn't feel so brave. *What if the dog sees me? What if it tries to catch me?* She glanced back to the warren. *Maybe I should forget about the dome and go straight home.* She sat as still as a statue … thinking hard … trying to decide. She had to make up her mind. And quick!

To the dome?

To the warren?

To the dome?

She took a deep bunny breath. Yes! To the dome!

Without wasting another moment, off she hopped—straight for the dome.

The closer she got, the curiouser she got. At the edge of the dark pine forest, Baby Baklava stopped to catch her breath. To her surprise, she'd stopped right beside a half-hidden sparkly-wrapped egg. She smiled when she thought of all the eggs she and the Biscotti bunnies had hidden for the Easter egg hunt. She picked it up. *I'll put it where it'll be easier for the children to find*, she said to herself. She was about to set it down in a new spot when she stopped. She turned the egg over and over in her paws.

It *looked* like a Biscotti egg.

It *felt* like a Biscotti egg.

But …

But it didn't *smell*
like a Biscotti egg!

No! It smelled yucky! How could this be?
What had happened? *I don't want the children
finding a yucky egg*, she muttered to herself.
*After I've checked out the dome, I'll take it back to
the warren.*

Baby B tucked the egg under her paw and
hopped farther into the forest. She could
see the dome clearly now and, as she got
closer, she noticed something on the roof.
It was about her size, it had straight-up ears,
and it was brown, like her. It looked sorta'
like a bunny! A funny bunny! She waved and
called out, "Hello! Are you friendly?"

The funny bunny waved back and then,
suddenly, jumped off the roof. He landed
upside down on the ground. His hat and
bunny ears fell off, and so did the egg he
was hiding under his hat. He'd quickly
tucked the egg back in his hat and put it and
the bunny ears back on.

Before Baby B could yell "Hello" again, the funny bunny appeared at her side, looking a bit rumpled.

Baby B said, "I'm Baby Baklava. Who are you?"

"I'm Ralph." He pointed to the dome. "That's where I live."

"I live in B&B Warren, over there." She pointed back across the meadow. "I spotted your dome house when my brothers and sisters and cousins and I were hiding Easter eggs. My papa is Sir Bentley Biscotti. He's the *official* Easter bunny. He was knighted by the Queen of the Fairies." She stepped closer to Ralph and studied him up and down, from the top of his straight-up ears to the toes of his shiny black boots. "Are you a real bunny? Do you know about the Easter egg hunt? Why were you on the roof?"

"Whoa!" Ralph raised one hand like he was stopping traffic. "One question at a time." He cleared his throat. "I guess you could say I'm a bunny—for now. Yes, I know about the hunt, and I was on the roof because I couldn't sleep."

"I couldn't sleep either. I was too curious about your dome house. I wanted to find out if it was friendly or not."

"*I'm* friendly," Ralph said, "but … but—"

"Me, too!" Baby Baklava burst in, "and now that we're friends, you can call me Baby B. Can I see inside your house?"

Ralph shook his head. "Uh … I don't think that's a good idea. Mugsy gets very grumpy if you wake him up." What Ralph didn't say was that, until this very moment, he'd thought Mugsy was the *official* Easter bunny and that Mugsy's *eggs* were the *official* eggs.

All of a sudden, he was worried.

He was worried about the big switch-a-roo.

He was worried about Baby B telling her papa what Mugsy and the mogsters, including himself, had done.

And he was worried about Sir Biscotti's delicious chocolate egg hidden under his own red hat.

"Don't worry, I'll be as quiet as a mouse," whispered Baby B. "Who's Mugsy?"

"He owns the dome." Ralph pointed to the roof. "See those four big M's on the top? They stand for Mugsy Maldoom's Marvelous Mogadome."

"It *is* marvelous! exclaimed Baby B. She grabbed Ralph's arm and pulled him toward the dome. "I can't wait to meet Mr. Mugsy. Then, I have to get back to the warren to show my papa this." She held up the sparkly-wrapped egg. "I just found it. It *looks* like the eggs we hid, but it's *not* like our Biscotti eggs at all." She held it under Ralph's nose. "Smell. It's sooo stinky. The children won't like it one bit."

Ralph gulped. He knew that smell.

And he knew all of Mugsy's eggs smelled like that.

And he knew about Mugsy's plan to become the official Easter Bunny.

And he knew the Easter egg hunt would now be spoiled.

And, worst of all, he knew he couldn't do anything about it.

"C'mon," Baby B urged. "I'll meet Mr. Mugsy and then— "

And then she heard a woof. She spun around and there, in the meadow, not far away, was the very same dog that had poked its nose in the warren. "Oh, no!" she cried, grabbing Ralph's arm. "I've got to get back home before that nosy dog sees me! I don't think he likes bunnies. C'mon!"

Ralph didn't stop to argue. He wasn't about to find out if the dog likes mogsters. With Baby B leading the way, the two new friends raced straight back to the warren.

Meanwhile, with his nosy nose to the ground …

HELP! Easter Bunny is in Trouble

CHAPTER 11

Meanwhile, with his nosy nose to the ground, Truffle sniffed out more and more smelly eggs.

"Oh, no, they're *all* stinky!" Tulip moaned. "What's happened?"

"Easta' Bunny make icky eggs," Washington said.

Tulip shook her head. "No, Washington, Easter Bunny *doesn't* make icky eggs. Somebody *else* makes icky eggs." She scratched her head. "But who?"

Washington's bottom lip began to quiver. "Easta' Bunny not nice. Me no yike."

Tulip patted her little brother's head. "It'll be okay, Washington. I don't know what's happened, but one thing I know for sure— this can't be the Easter Bunny's fault. It just can't be."

But, whose fault is it? she wondered. *Who'd play such a mean, nasty trick on the Easter Bunny?*

And I'm worried about all those children who can't wait to find their eggs.

Tulip looked around for Truffle. She spotted him up ahead, running here and there, back and forth, his nose to the ground. Then, suddenly, he stopped, turned around, and scrambled back to Tulip. He sat down on her foot, looked up at her, and yipped. This time Tulip didn't hesitate. She knew exactly what Truffle was saying in his basset hound way—*Follow me, Tulip, follow me!*

She grabbed Washington's hand. "He wants to show us something. C'mon!"

Tulip and Washington chased after Truffle. Little did they know that the floppy-eared basset hound had picked up *another* scent—the scent of Baby B.

It was where she stopped to look at the dome.

It was where Baby B waved to Ralph.

It was where Baby B and Ralph became friends.

And it was where Tulip and Washington now stood.

Tulip's eyes popped wide open. So did Washington's. "Yook, Tooyip!" He pointed straight ahead. "Yook!"

"I'm yooking," Tulip said, "and I don't yike what I see." She took hold of her little brother's hand. "I see trouble, Washington. *Big* trouble."

Meanwhile, back at the warren ...

CHAPTER 12

Meanwhile, back at the warren, Baby B and Ralph had scampered as quickly as their little legs could carry them, straight into the entrance. Once safely inside, they stopped to catch their breath.

"Whew! That was close," panted Baby B.

Ralph nodded. "Too close." He looked around. "This is where you live?"

Baby Baklava nodded. "Me and Mama and Papa and my 10 brothers and sisters and lots of aunts and uncles and lots and lots of cousins. We're the Biscottis, the *official* Easter Bunny family. Want to meet everybody?"

"I … I … guess so," stuttered Ralph. He only knew other mogsters, so meeting bunnies made him nervous.

"Follow me." Still clutching the stinky egg, Baby B hopped off down the tunnel. She passed the room where her mama and papa were still asleep and ended up at the room where she'd left the other bunnies munching on the green hay and broccoli treats. She peeked inside. Not a bunny was to be seen. "Hmmm, I wonder where everybody is?" She thought for a moment. "I bet I know!" She took off down another tunnel with Ralph close behind. She stopped at a door that said FUN AND GAMES.

Ralph peeked in. The FUN AND GAMES room was chock-a-block with bunnies—chattering, laughing, playing bunnies. "What're they doing?" Ralph asked.

"Having fun. There are lots of things to do."

"Like what?" Ralph asked.

"Well, you can hop on trampolines, jump rope, play video games, read books, play checkers, watch TV, play hopscotch, do crossword puzzles, hula hoop, call your friends on your cell phone, paint—"

"Whoa!" Ralph butted in. "That's a lotta' things, and I've never heard about any of 'em."

"Don't you have a FUN AND GAMES room in the dome?"

Ralph shook his head. "I wish. It looks pretty cool."

"It's *very* cool. My favorite book is "*The Tale of Peter Rabbit*," and my favorite video game is *Angry Bunnies*. Wanna' play?"

"I … I think I'll just watch first." Not only did Ralph have no idea how to play a video game, he didn't even know what it was. And he felt too embarrassed to admit it.

"No problemo." Baby Baklava looked Ralph over, up and down, front to back. "Do you have a cell phone?"

"Uh … cell phone? No, I don't have one of those."

"Never mind. We've got extras." Without another word, she led Ralph to a box filled with cell phones. She put down the stinky egg and handed him a phone. "I'll show you how it works. Easy-peasy."

Ralph caught on fast.

"It's yours to keep," said Baby B. "We can call each other when you're back at the dome."

"Gee, thanks." He looked around the room. "That jumpy trampoline thingy looks fun. Can we do that?"

"No problemo. We can do it together, but first I'll hide this stinky egg in the box under all the cell phones."

After lots of trampoline jumping, hula hooping, and several games of checkers, Ralph thanked Baby B for showing him the FUN AND GAMES room and headed for the door. "I'd better get back before Mugsy discovers I'm gone."

Baby B nodded. "Watch out for that dog. Doesn't look very friendly." She and Ralph scampered down the long tunnel that led back to the entrance. "Call me when you get to the dome."

As she watched her new friend scurry back across the meadow, she suddenly remembered the smelly egg she'd left in the FUN AND GAMES room. *Wait until Papa finds out,* she thought. *Maybe Mama made a big egg-making mistake. Maybe the Biscottis won't be the official Easter egg family any more.* Those thoughts brought tears to Baby B's eyes.

The egg was right where she'd left it. She picked it up and headed out the door, down the tunnel toward her parents' room. *They're going to be so upset. It's almost time for the hunt, and all those children will ...* "Wait!" she said out loud, stopping short in her tracks. "It's just *one* egg. I'll hide it, and no one will ever know. No problemo."

Baby B hopped back to the FUN AND GAMES room and hid the stinky egg on the highest shelf where no one would ever think to look. Then she decided to play her favorite video game, *Angry Bunnies*. Soon, she forgot all about the egg.

Meanwhile, outside the Mogadome ...

CHAPTER 13

Meanwhile, outside the Mogadome, Tulip and Washington Twinkle were staring in shock and wonder at what they saw—Mugsy Maldoom's Marvelous Mogadome!

"Mugsy!" Tulip exclaimed. "How did *he* get here?"

"Gwumpy Mugsy," said Washington. "Me no yike."

"Me neither," Tulip added. "Remember how he tried to ruin Santa's presents last Christmas? Now, I bet he's trying to ruin the Easter Bunny's eggs. What a sneaky meanie."

"Neaky meanie," Washington repeated. "Me go home."

Tulip grabbed her little brother's hand. "No way. We can't go home. Not yet. We don't have much time, but we have to find out what Mugsy is up to. We're paying a visit to the Mogadome, right now!"

On their tiptoes, Tulip and Washington, followed by Truffle, crept up to the Mogadome. "There are no windows, so I can't peek in," Tulip whispered, "and I don't see a door, either."

While Tulip was searching for a door, Truffle was sniffing. And sniffing. Suddenly, he stopped sniffing and began yipping. "Shhh, Truffle," Tulip said, putting her finger to her lips. "We don't want Mugsy to know we're here."

Too late!

A hidden door suddenly flew open, right where Truffle was sniffing and yipping. And who should step out but ...

Tulip squinted. "Easter Bunny? Is that you?" She stepped closer. "Wait a minute." She parked her hands on her hips and shook her head. "*You're* not the Easter Bunny. You're ..."

Washington ducked behind Tulip and peeked out between her legs "Mugsy!" he yelled. "Gwumpy Mugsy!"

"Well, well, well. Look who's come to visit. Three-lips, Four-lips—"

"*Tu*lip!" snapped Tulip. "You still can't think straight, can you? And you look ridiculous with your fake bunny ears and your fake bunny suit. Everyone can see you're not the *real* Easter Bunny."

"Is that so? Who do you think made hundreds of eggs for the hunt? Me, that's who. The *new, official* Easter Bunny." He held out the smelly sock that hung around his neck. "See? I've been knighted. So there!"

Tulip scoffed. "Knighted? Who knighted you?"

"Me. I knighted me."

Tulip snickered. "You can't knight yourself. Everybody knows that. Only the Queen of Fairies can—"

Mugsy puffed up his chest and stepped closer to Tulip. "And I have dozens of beautiful egg-making machines for making my special-formula, secret-surprise, ultra-gourmet Easter eggs. The children will *love* them. Guaranteed."

Tulip rolled her eyes. "No way. Your so-called special-formula, secret-surprise, ultra-gourmet eggs are stinky and disgusting."

While Tulip and Mugsy were arguing about knight-hooding and egg-making, Washington spotted something shiny on the ground. He picked it up. "For my coyection," he murmured and slipped a shiny key into his pocket. It was the very same key that had dropped out of Ralph's hat when he jumped off the roof of the Mogadome.

"And no one will like *your* eggs," Tulip continued. "They're—"

"Yucky," Washington broke in. "Me no yike." He tugged on Tulip's jacket. "Me go home, *now!*"

"Okay, Washington, we'll go home …" she paused and looked directly at the chubby troll, "but not until we find out what Mugsy, the *fake* Easter Bunny, is up to."

HELP! Easter Bunny is in Trouble

CHAPTER 14

"I'll show you exactly what I'm up to," Mugsy said, puffing out his chest. "Follow me."

Tulip took Washington's hand, and they followed the meanie troll into the Mogadome. Truffle trotted behind.

Mugsy led the Twinkles into a huge room. Lined up along the walls were dozens of egg-making machines the size of refrigerators. Each one was decorated with *fak*e sparkly gems, and each one had a door with bars. The bars were far enough apart to see inside but too close together to crawl through. Besides the egg-making machines, there were huge bins. They also had doors with bars that were far enough apart to see inside but too close together to crawl through. "Look at my machines," said the troll proudly. "They're my beauties."

"Stinky booties," said Washington.

Tulip wrinkled her nose. "What's that smell?"

Mugsy rubbed his chubby tummy and grinned. "The delicious smell of my super-special secret ingredients."

"Secret ingredients?" Tulip repeated. "What secret ingredients?"

Mugsy sniggered. "You'll never guess, but since you'll never escape from my Mogadome, I'll tell you. Garlic and fish oil. Yum."

"Garlic and fish oil!" Tulip exclaimed.

"Yessiree! Because of me, Sir Mugsy Maldoom, Easter eggs will never be the same. Children will love me and my garlic-and-fish-oil eggs much more than Sir Bentley Biscotti and his boring ol' chocolate eggs. And I'll be famous. Super famous. Want one?"

Tulip pinched her nose. "No, thanks. And no one else will want one either ... not even Truffle." She remembered Truffle's stinky breath after he chomped on the egg in the meadow. It smelled just like garlic and fish oil! *So, that's it*, Tulip said to herself. *Mugsy is trying to ruin the Easter Bunny just like he tried to ruin Santa. We've got to stop him ... but how?*

Tulip didn't have much time to think. Soon, the sun would peek over the horizon and the Easter egg hunt would begin. And the children would find Mugsy's disgusting eggs instead of the real Easter Bunny's delicious ones. *Until I figure out what to do, I'll pretend I love his egg-making machines*, she said to herself. She smiled sweetly at the troll. "Your machines *are* beautiful, Mugsy. Could we get a closer look, pleeeze?"

"Ah, I knew you'd love my beauties. Follow me."

Tulip, Washington, and Truffle followed closely behind the troll. As he led them passed the huge bins, she noticed two things:

> (1) Some of the bins were filled with eggs, and…

> (2) *All* the eggs in the bins had **OEB** stickers on them.

Tulip knew **OEB** stood for **O**fficial **E**aster **B**unny, but silly Mugsy didn't know. *So, that's it. Mugsy stole Sir Biscotti's real **OEB** eggs and put his own stinky ones in their place! But I can't let him know I've figured out his ridiculous plan.* She cleared her throat and asked, "Why are there stickers on the eggs in the bins?"

"Oh … uh … um … those eggs are for … uh … next year," Mugsy stuttered. "I like to plan ahead to be sure every precious little girl and boy will get one of my special eggs." He hurried past the bins and stopped beside an empty jewel-covered egg-making machine. "Wanna see inside, Miss Nosey Posey?"

Tulip peeked inside. "I don't think—" she began, but before she could finish her sentence, Mugsy pushed her into the machine. Then, he pushed Washington and Truffle in, too. Before the three Twinkles could hop out, Mugsy slammed the door shut and locked it.

"Me out! Me out!" cried Washington.

"Woof, woof," woofed Truffle.

Tulip pushed on the bars on the door. "You won't get away with this, Mugsy. I know what you're up to. You tried to spoil Christmas and Santa, and now you're trying to spoil Easter and the Easter Bunny. It'll never work."

Tulip sounded brave, but her heart sank as she watched the troll skip away singing, "Hippity-hop, hippity-hop, Easter's on its way."

"I'm afraid we're in trouble, Washington. Big trouble."

Meanwhile …

HELP! Easter Bunny is in Trouble

CHAPTER 15

Meanwhile, after meeting Baby Baklava and all her many relatives, and after learning how to play checkers and how to use a cell phone, and after racing back to the safety of the Mogadome, Ralph was starving. Quick as a wink, he dashed back up to the roof, sat down, and pulled out the Sir-Bentley-**OEB** egg he'd hidden under his hat. He took a bite. It was so delicious that, before he knew it, he'd gobbled up the entire egg. *I wish I had another one*, he thought. *I could eat 10 more. There's lots of Mugsy's eggs hidden in the meadow, but Mugsy's eggs aren't delicious like Sir Bentley's. And Sir Bentley's are all locked up in the bins.*

With his stomach grumbling for more chocolate, Ralph gazed hungrily over the meadow. Suddenly, he stood up. *Wait a minute!* He bonked himself on the head. *I forgot! I have a key! I have a key! I can help myself to as many eggs as I want!*

Quicker than it takes to say "Baby Baklava," Ralph jumped off the mogadome roof and scampered inside. He slipped off his hat to get the key he'd hidden there. But … but … where was the key? He turned his hat upside down. He shook it. He felt inside and shook it again.

Just then, he heard a voice. It came from the far end of the dome. It wasn't Mugsy, and it wasn't another mogster. He tip-toed toward the sound. He heard someone yell, "Me out! Me out!" followed by "Woof, woof."

Ralph ducked out of sight and peeked out from behind a machine. Here's what he saw: Inside one of the egg-making machines was the same dog he'd seen in the meadow. And the dog wasn't alone. There was also a girl and a boy. *What are they doing here?* he wondered. *They'd better get out before Mugsy finds them.* Ralph crept closer to get a better look.

Meanwhile …

CHAPTER 16

Meanwhile, locked inside the jewel-covered egg-making machine, Truffle was woofing, Washington was crying, and Tulip was trying to figure out what to do. Again and again, she pushed as hard as she could on the bars, but it was no use. She sighed. "It's almost time for the Easter egg hunt, and we're trapped in here. The children will be so sad when they bite into Mugsy's yucky eggs."

"Yucky eggs," Washington repeated.

"We can't let Mugsy spoil Easter like he tried to spoil Christmas. We just can't." Tulip pushed on the door again. "If we just had a key, we could—"

"Me key, Tooyip," Washington butted in.

"You're not a key, Washington. I mean, we *need* a key, a real key, to unlock this dumb door."

"Me weal key," Washington repeated a little louder.

Tulip sighed heavily. "Okay, so you're a key."

"*Me* not key. Yook."

Tulip turned to look at Washington. He was holding a key. "Me *find* key."

Tulip grabbed the key. "Maybe it fits the machine! If it does, you're brilliant, Washington!"

"Me bwillant," said Washington, grinning.

Without a moment's hesitation, Tulip reached through the bars on the door and fitted the key into the lock.

Click! The door swung open!

In a flash, out jumped the three Twinkles. Tulip high-fived her little brother. "But we still have a big problem. How do we put Sir Bentley's **OEB**-eggs back where they belong? If we don't do something quickly, the children will find Mugsy's disgusting eggs, and the Easter hunt will be ruined!"

While the Twinkles were escaping from the machine, and Tulip was wondering how they could save the children from garlic-and-fish-oil eggs, Ralph had watched and heard every word. *So that's where my key is*, he thought. *And that's why Mugsy made us do the big switch-a-roo. That wasn't very nice.*

Ralph stepped out from behind a machine. "Ahem," he said. "I'm Ralph. Maybe I can help."

Tulip's eyes popped wide open. "But ... but ... aren't you one of Mugsy's mogsters?"

"Yes, but I'm not like the others. For starters, I have a new friend, Baby Baklava and—"

"Baby Baklava," Tulip repeated. "Who is—?"

"She's one of Easter Bunny's 11 children, and I know all about Mugsy's egg switch-a-roo 'cause I helped do the switch-a-roo, and I think Mugsy's eggs are yucky, and I love Easter Bunny's chocolate ones, and—"

"Whoa! Hold on a minute," Tulip said. "You said you helped with the egg switch-a-roo?"

Ralph nodded. "And then Baby B took me to the *official* Easter Bunny's warren where she lives, and she taught me how to play checkers and how to use a cell phone, and—"

"Whoa! Hold on another minute," Tulip butted in again. "You mean you *have* a cell phone?"

Ralph nodded and pulled it out of his pocket.

Tulip's eyes lit up. "Can you call Baby B at the *official* Easter Bunny's warren?"

Ralph nodded again.

"Then I have an idea. It just may save the Easter egg hunt after all." Tulip bent down and whispered something in the mogster's ear. Ralph smiled and pulled out his cell phone.

CHAPTER 17

Ralph smiled and pulled out his cell phone from under his hat. He called Baby Baklava. Tulip watched in amazement, not just because a mogster had a cell phone, but because he knew just who to call.

"Hello, Baby B. This is Ralph."

Pause.

"Yes, I remembered how to use my cell phone."

Pause.

"Yes, I'm calling from the Mogadome."

Pause.

"Yes, we need your help."

Long pause.

"Yes, we need you and your brothers and sisters and cousins and all your friends to pick up Mugsy's stinky eggs and bring them back here, ASAP."

Short pause.

"Yes, every last one. Thanks, Baby B. Bye."

Ralph stuck his cell phone back under his hat. "The Biscotti bunnies are filling up their wagons and wheelbarrows and backpacks. They'll be here in just a few minutes."

Tulip grinned. "Fantastic!" But, quickly, her grin turned into a frown. "Wait! I'm still confused. You're one of Mugsy's mogsters. He's a grumpy ol' meanie; I thought his mogsters would also be grumpy meanies. So, why are you helping us?"

"Well," said Ralph, "first, I learned that Mugsy isn't the *real, official* Easter Bunny …

"and then I had a taste of a delicious chocolate Easter egg made by the *real official* Easter Bunny …

"and then I met Baby Baklava and her huge family of bunnies …

"and then she told me *her* dad is the official Easter Bunny …

"and then she didn't like the smell of Mugsy's egg that she found in the meadow and that I helped put there …

"and then she taught me how to use a cell phone …

"and then I—"

"Whoa! Stop!" Tulip burst out. "They're here!" She gazed in wonder at Baby B's huge family of bunnies with their wagons and wheelbarrows and backpacks filled to the brims with Mugsy's stinky eggs.

At the front of the crowd stood Baby B. Ralph rushed over to her. Tulip, Washington, and Truffle followed close behind.

"This is my new friend, Baby Baklava," said Ralph.

"So nice to meet you," said Tulip. "Thank you for helping us. Please come with me into the mogadome. We've got to hurry."

Once inside, Tulip told the bunnies the three things they needed to do:

"First, all those icky eggs you collected—dump them into the empty egg-making machines. They're the ones with all those fake gems.

"Second: Fill your wagons and wheelbarrows and backpacks with the real **OEB**'s eggs. They're locked in these big bins behind me.

"Third: Hide the **OEB**'s eggs again, right where you did before. And please, please hurry!"

Baby Baklava nodded her long bunny ears. "No problemo. Leave it to us."

In short order, the bunnies grabbed every one of Mugsy's stinky eggs and dumped them into the empty egg-making machines.

Quickly, Tulip used the key Washington had found to unlock the bins. Then, faster than Ralph could tell the Twinkles *every single thing* about the FUN AND GAMES room, the Biscotti bunnies filled their wagons and wheelbarrows and backpacks with the **OEB**'s eggs.

In double-quick time, the Biscotti bunnies raced to re-hide every last delicious, chocolate egg in Lilac Village and in the green meadow. Then, they scurried back to the warren to continue playing in the FUN AND GAMES room.

Baby Baklava called Ralph to tell him the deed was done.

"Thank you, Baby B. The Twinkles thank you, too. Bye."

"You're our hero, Ralph," said Tulip. "You and the bunnies helped us save the Easter egg hunt. Now, we Twinkles had better—"

At that moment, a voice boomed from the Mogadome. "YOU'D BETTER *WHAT?*"

CHAPTER 18

"YOU'D BETTER WHAT?" Mugsy boomed again.

"Uh-oh," gulped Tulip.

"Uh-oh," gulped Washington.

"Uh-oh," gulped Ralph.

Tulip swallowed a second gulp. "Oh, hi, Mugsy," she said, smiling sweetly. "We LOVED our stay in your beautiful machine, but we think we'd better get back home now."

She paused and stepped closer to the troll. "I don't mean to be rude, but for someone who has been knighted, you look a bit scruffy. Your ears are on backwards, your cotton balls are falling off, and ... and ... "She leaned closer. "Where's your black olive nose? "

"I ate it," the troll muttered. "I got hungry."

"If you're still hungry, I happen to know where there are tons of yummy-in-the-tummy garlic-and-fish-oil eggs." Tulip pointed to the machines in the Mogadome. "They're all yours."

Mugsy looked to where Tulip pointed. "But ... but ... how—?"

"It doesn't matter. All that matters is that the children will find delicious, chocolatey eggs in the hunt this morning."

Tulip stepped up even closer to the troll. "By the way, you can take off that smelly sock around your neck. It looks silly, and besides, no one believes you got it from the Queen of the Fairies."

"Fairies, schmairies," Mugsy muttered, pulling off the sock. "Forget about fairies. Forget about bunnies. Forget about eggs. I'm going to make myself a gallon of delicious onion juice, and then I'm going to soak in a beautiful mud bath." He wobbled back across the Mogadome.

"You mean you don't want to take over Easter Bunny's business after all?" Tulip called after him.

Mugsy didn't answer, but as he disappeared behind a huge bin, Tulip heard him mutter, "Business, schmisness! I'm sick of the Easter bunny. I'll be the *Tooth Fairy*! The children will love me—*me, me, me*. I'll be the *best ...*"

Tulip didn't wait around to hear Mugsy's new plan. She grabbed Washington by the hand and Truffle by his red-plaid scarf. "C'mon. Let's get outta' here before he changes his mind about the Easter Bunny."

The three Twinkles headed across the meadow. Suddenly, Tulip stopped. She turned and looked back. Ralph was standing all by himself in front of the Mogadome. He looked so sad and lonely. "What are *you* going to do?" called Tulip.

Ralph shrugged. "Don't know. If Mugsy finds out what I did, he'll … "

Tulip felt a tug on her jacket. "What, Washington?"

"Baby B yike," said her little brother.

"Ralph isn't yike a bunny," Tulip said.

"*Baby B yike Walf*," Washington repeated, louder.

"Sorry, Washington," began his big sister, "but I don't get—"

"*I* get it!" Ralph cried. "Baby B likes *me*! Do you think she … ?"

Washington jumped up and down. "Yes! Call Baby B! Call Baby B!"

"Great idea!" Ralph pulled out his phone and tapped in some numbers. "Hi, Baby B. This is Ralph."

Pause

"I was just wondering if … uh, if it would it be okay if I uh—?

Pause

"Are you sure?"

Pause

"Even if I'm not a *real* bunny?"

Long pause

"Now? Right now?"

Short pause.

"Fantastic! I'm on my way!" He waved to Washington. "Thanks, Buddy. Bye bye, Twinkles."

Washington and Tulip watched and waved as Ralph sprinted across the meadow and out of sight.

"Me yike Baby B and Walf," Washington said.

"Me, too." Tulip grabbed her little brother's hand and pulled him into a run. "Yook, Washington. The sun's coming up. We better get home before Mom discovers our empty beds. There's no time to spare."

CHAPTER 19

"There's no time to spare, kids," Mrs. Twinkle called softly. "Time to get up and get dressed. The Easter egg hunt's about to begin."

Little did Mrs. Twinkle know that, under their blankets, the kids were already dressed. They were just pretending to be asleep.

Little did Mrs. Twinkle know that, in his comfy donut-shaped bed, the basset hound was already wearing his red-plaid scarf. He was just pretending to be asleep.

Little did Mrs.. Twinkle know that Tulip and Washington and Truffle were all ready for the best Easter egg hunt ever.

The End

HELP! Easter Bunny is in Trouble

We hope that you enjoyed this title and look forward to many more to come. Please, leave us a review! Reviews matter to all of our authors.

Take a look at some of our other award-winning series at https://threeravenspublishing.com/series-universes/

Visit us at https://www.threeravenspublishing.com and sign up for our newsletter for the latest and greatest news on upcoming titles and events.

Other series and titles you might enjoy.

You can also keep up to date with our latest release announcements on Scifi.radio and get some of the best fandom programing on the planet.

Scifi for your Wifi

And don't forget to check out the latest edition of **Car Wars**

http://www.sjgames.com/car-wars/

Or the other amazing titles from
Steve Jackson Games

http://www.sjgames.com

...or the latest in the Car Warriors: Autoduel Chronicle fiction series.
https://threeravenspublishing.com/car-warriors-autoduel-chronicles/

www.ingramcontent.com/pod-product-compliance
Lightning Source LLC
Chambersburg PA
CBHW020323130626
46549CB00003B/987